AFTERMATH

AFTERMATH

BY
HENRY WADSWORTH LONGFELLOW

1873

WORDWELL
enterprises

CONTENTS

TALES OF A WAYSIDE INN

PART THIRD

PRELUDE

THE evening came; the golden vane
A moment in the sunset glanced,
Then darkened, and then gleamed again,
As from the east the moon advanced
And touched it with a softer light;
While underneath, with flowing mane,
Upon the sign the Red Horse pranced,
And galloped forth into the night.

But brighter than the afternoon
That followed the dark day of rain,
And brighter than the golden vane
That glistened in the rising moon,
Within the ruddy firelight gleamed;
And every separate window-pane,
Backed by the outer darkness, showed
A mirror, where the flamelets gleamed
And flickered to and fro, and seemed
A bonfire lighted in the road.

Amid the hospitable glow,
Like an old actor on the stage,
With the uncertain voice of age,
The singing chimney chanted low
The homely songs of long ago.

The voice that Ossian heard of yore,
When midnight winds were in his hall;
A ghostly and appealing call,
A sound of days that are no more!

And dark as Ossian sat the Jew,
And listened to the sound, and knew
The passing of the airy hosts,
The gray and misty cloud of ghosts
In their interminable flight ;
And listening muttered in his beard,
With accent indistinct and weird,
"Who are ye, children of the Night?"

Beholding his mysterious face,
"Tell me," the gay Sicilian said,
"Why was it that in breaking bread
At supper, you bent down your head
And, musing, paused a little space,
As one who says a silent grace?"

The Jew replied, with solemn air,
"I said the Manichæan's prayer.
It was his faith, —perhaps is mine,—
That life in all its forms is one,
And that its secret conduits run
Unseen, but in unbroken line,
From the great fountain-head divine
Through man and beast, through grain and grass.

Howe'er we struggle, strive, and cry,
From death there can be no escape,
And no escape from life, alas!
Because we cannot die, but pass
From one into another shape:
It is but into life we die.

"Therefore the Manichæan said
This simple prayer on breaking bread,
Lest he with hasty hand or knife

Might wound the incarcerated life,
The soul in things that we call dead:
'I did not reap thee, did not bind thee,
I did not thrash thee, did not grind thee,
Nor did I in the oven bake thee!
It was not I, it was another
Did these things unto thee, O brother;
I only have thee, hold thee, break thee!'"

"That birds have souls I can concede,"
The poet cried, with glowing cheeks;
"The flocks that from their beds of reed
Uprising north or southward fly,
And flying write upon the sky
The biforked letter of the Greeks,
As hath been said by Rucellai;
All birds that sing or chirp or cry,
Even those migratory bands,
The minor poets of the air,
The plover, peep, and sanderling,
That hardly can be said to sing,
But pipe along the barren sands,—
All these have souls akin to ours;
So hath the lovely race of flowers:
Thus much I grant, but nothing more.
The rusty hinges of a door
Are not alive because they creak;
This chimney, with its dreary roar,
These rattling windows, do not speak!"
"To me they speak," the Jew replied;
"And in the sounds that sink and soar,
I hear the voices of a tide
That breaks upon an unknown shore!"

Here the Sicilian interfered:
"That was your dream, then, as you dozed
A moment since, with eyes half-closed,
And murmured something in your beard."
The Hebrew smiled, and answered, "Nay;
Not that, but something very near;
Like, and yet not the same, may seem
The vision of my waking dream;
Before it wholly dies away,
Listen to me, and you shall hear."

THE SPANISH JEW'S TALE

AZRAEL.

KING SOLOMON, before his palace gate
At evening, on the pavement tesselate
Was walking with a stranger from the East,
Arrayed in rich attire as for a feast,
The mighty Runjeet-Sing, a learned man,
And Rajah of the realms of Hindostan.
And as they walked the guest became aware
Of a white figure in the twilight air,
Gazing intent, as one who with surprise
His form and features seemed to recognize;
And in a whisper to the king he said:
"What is yon shape, that, pallid as the dead,
Is watching me, as if he sought to trace
In the dim light the features of my face?"
The king looked, and replied: "I know him well;
It is the Angel men call Azrael,
'Tis the Death Angel; what hast thou to fear?'
And the guest answered: "Lest he should come near,
And speak to me, and take away my breath!
Save me from Azrael, save me from death!
O king, that hast dominion o'er the wind,
Bid it arise and bear me hence to Ind."

The king gazed upward at the cloudless sky,
Whispered a word, and raised his hand on high,
And lo! the signet-ring of chrysoprase
On his uplifted finger seemed to blaze
With hidden fire, and rushing from the west

There came a mighty wind, and seized the guest
And lifted him from earth, and on they passed,
His shining garments streaming in the blast,
A silken banner o'er the walls upreared,
A purple cloud, that gleamed and disappeared.
Then said the Angel, smiling: "If this man
Be Rajah Runjeet-Sing of Hindostan,
Thou hast done well in listening to his prayer;
I was upon my way to seek him there."

INTERLUDE

"O EDREHI, forbear to-night
Your ghostly legends of affright,
And let the Talmud rest in peace;
Spare us your dismal tales of death
That almost take away one's breath;
So doing, may your tribe increase."

Thus the Sicilian said; then went
And on the spinnet's rattling keys
Played Marianina, like a breeze
From Naples and the Southern seas,
That brings us the delicious scent
Of citron and of orange trees,
And memories of soft days of ease
At Capri and Amalfi spent.

"Not so," the eager Poet said;
"At least, not so before I tell
The story of my Azrael,
An angel mortal as ourselves,
Which in an ancient tome I found
Upon a convent's dusty shelves,
Chained with an iron chain, and bound
In parchment, and with clasps of brass,
Lest from its prison, some dark day,
It might be stolen or steal away,
While the good friars were singing mass.

"It is a tale of Charlemagne,
When like a thunder-cloud, that lowers
And sweeps from mountain-crest to coast,
With lightning flaming through its showers,
He swept across the Lombard plain,
Beleaguering with his warlike train
Pavía, the country's pride and boast,
The City of the Hundred Towers."

Thus heralded the tale began,
And thus in sober measure ran.

THE POET'S TALE

CHARLEMAGNE.

OLGER the Dane and Desiderio,
King of the Lombards, on a lofty tower
Stood gazing northward o'er the rolling plains,
League after league of harvests, to the foot
Of the snow-crested Alps, and saw approach
A mighty army, thronging all the roads
That led into the city. And the King
Said unto Olger, who had passed his youth
As hostage at the court of France, and knew
The Emperor's form and face: "Is Charlemagne
Among that host?" And Olger answered: "No."

And still the innumerable multitude
Flowed onward and increased, until the King
Cried in amazement: "Surely Charlemagne
Is coming in the midst of all these knights!'
And Olger answered slowly: "No; not yet;
He will not come so soon." Then much disturbed
King Desiderio asked: "What shall we do,
If he approach with a still greater army?"
And Olger answered: "When he shall appear,
You will behold what manner of man he is;
But what will then befall us I know not."

Then came the guard that never knew repose,
The Paladins of France; and at the sight
The Lombard King o'ercome with terror cried :
"This must be Charlemagne!" and as before
Did Olger answer: "No; not yet, not yet."

And then appeared in panoply complete
The Bishops and the Abbots and the Priests
Of the imperial chapel, and the Counts;
And Desiderio could no more endure
The light of day, nor yet encounter death,
But sobbed aloud and said: "Let us go down
And hide us in the bosom of the earth,
Far from the sight and anger of a foe
So terrible as this!" And Olger said:
"When you behold the harvests in the fields
Shaking with fear, the Po and the Ticino
Lashing the city walls with iron waves,
Then may you know that Charlemagne is come."
And even as he spake, in the northwest,
Lo! there uprose a black and threatening cloud,
Out of whose bosom flashed the light of arms
Upon the people pent up in the city;
A light more terrible than any darkness;
And Charlemagne appeared; —a Man of Iron!

IIis helmet was of iron, and his gloves
Of iron, and his breastplate and his greaves
And tassets were of iron, and his shield.
In his left hand he held an iron spear,
In his right hand his sword invincible.
The horse he rode on had the strength of iron,
And color of iron. All who went before him,
Beside him and behind him, his whole host,
Were armed with iron, and their hearts within them
Were stronger than the armor that they wore.
The fields and all the roads were filled with iron,
And points of iron glistened in the sun
And shed a terror through the city streets.

This at a single glance Olger the Dane
Saw from the tower, and turning to the King
Exclaimed in haste: "Behold! this is the man
You looked for with such eagerness!" and then
Fell as one dead at Desiderio's feet.

INTERLUDE

WELL pleased all listened to the tale,
That drew, the Student said, its pith
And marrow from the ancient myth
Of some one with an iron flail;
Or that portentous Man of Brass.
Hephaestus made in days of yore,
Who stalked about the Cretan shore,
And saw the ships appear and pass,
And threw stones at the Argonauts,
Being filled with indiscriminate ire
That tangled and perplexed his thoughts;
But, like a hospitable host,
When strangers landed on the coast,
Heated himself red-hot with fire,
And hugged them in his arms, and pressed
Their bodies to his burning breast.

The Poet answered: "No, not thus
The legend rose; it sprang at first
Out of the hunger and the thirst
In all men for the marvellous.
And thus it filled and satisfied
The imagination of mankind,
And this ideal to the mind
Was truer than historic fact.
Fancy enlarged and multiplied
The terrors of the awful name
Of Charlemagne, till he became

Armipotent in every act,
And, clothed in mystery, appeared
Not what men saw, but what they feared."

The Theologian said: "Perchance
Your chronicler in writing this
Had in his mind the Anabasis,
Where Xenophon describes the advance
Of Artaxerxes to the fight;
At first the low gray cloud of dust,
And then a blackness o'er the fields
As of a passing thunder-gust,
Then flash of brazen armor bright,
And ranks of men, and spears up-thrust,
Bowmen and troops with wicker shields,
And cavalry equipped in white,
And chariots ranged in front of these
With scythes upon their axle-trees."

To this the Student answered: "Well,
I also have a tale to tell
Of Charlemagne; a tale that throws
A softer light, more tinged with rose,
Than your grim apparition cast
Upon the darkness of the past.
Listen, and hear in English rhyme
What the good Monk of Lauresheim
Gives as the gossip of his time,
In mediæval Latin prose.'

THE STUDENT'S TALE

EMMA AND EGINHARD.

WHEN Alcuin taught the sons of Charlemagne,
In the free schools of Aix, how kings should reign,
And with them taught the children of the poor
How subjects should be patient and endure,
He touched the lips of some, as best befit,
With honey from the hives of Holy Writ;
Others intoxicated wtih the wine
Of ancient history, sweet but less divine;
Some with the wholesome fruits of grammar fed;
Others with mysteries of the stars o'erhead,
That hang suspended in the vaulted sky
Like lamps in some fair palace vast and high.

In sooth, it was a pleasant sight to sce
That Saxon monk, with hood and rosary,
With inkhorn at his belt, and pen and book,
And mingled love and reverence in his look,
Or hear the cloister and the court repeat
The measured footfalls of his sandaled feet,
Or watch him with the pupils of his school,
Gentle of speech, but absolute of rule.

Among them, always earliest in his place,
Was Eginhard, a youth of Frankish race,
Whose face was bright with flashes that forerun
The splendors of a yet unrisen sun.
To him all things were possible, and seemed
Not what he had accomplished, but had dreamed,
And what were tasks to others were his play,
The pastime of an idle holiday.

Smaragdo, Abbot of St. Michael's, said,
With many a shrug and shaking of the head,
Surely some demon must possess the lad,
Who showed more wit than ever school-boy had,
And learned his Trivium thus without the rod;
But Alcuin said it was the grace of God.

Thus he grew up, in Logic point-device,
Perfect in Grammar, and in Rhetoric nice;
Science of Numbers, Geometric art,
And lore of Stars, and Music knew by heart;
A Minnesinger, long before the times
Of those who sang their love in Suabian rhymes.

The Emperor, when he heard this good report
Of Eginhard much buzzed about the court,
Said to himself, "This stripling seems to be
Purposely sent into the world for me;
He shall become my scribe, and shall be schooled
In all the arts whereby the world is ruled."
Thus did the gentle Eginhard attain
To honor in the court of Charlemagne;
Became the sovereign's favorite, his right hand,
So that his fame was great in all the land,
And all men loved him for his modest grace
And comeliness of figure and of face.
An inmate of the palace, yet recluse,
A man of books, yet sacred from abuse
Among the armed knights with spur on heel,
The tramp of horses and the clang of steel;
And as the Emperor promised he was schooled
In all the arts by which the world is ruled.
But the one art supreme, whose law is fate,
The Emperor never dreamed of till too late.

Home from her convent to the palace came
The lovely Princess Emma, whose sweet name,
Whispered by seneschal or sung by bard,
Had often touched the soul of Eginhard.
He saw her from his window, as in state
She came, by knights attended through the gate;
He saw her at the banquet of that day,
Fresh as the morn, and beautiful as May;
He saw her in the garden, as she strayed
Among the flowers of summer with her maid,
And said to him, "O Eginhard, disclose
The meaning and the mystery of the rose";
And trembling he made answer: "In good sooth,
Its mystery is love, its meaning youth!"

How can I tell the signals and the signs
By which one heart another heart divines?
How can I tell the many thousand ways
By which it keeps the secret it betrays?

O mystery of love! O strange romance!
Among the Peers and Paladins of France,
Shining in steel, and prancing on gay steeds,
Noble by birth, yet nobler by great deeds,
The Princess Emma had no words nor looks
But for this clerk, this man of thought and books.

The summer passed, the autumn came; the stalks
Of lilies blackened in the garden walks;
The leaves fell, russet-golden and blood-red,
Love-letters thought the poet fancy-led,
Or Jove descending in a shower of gold
Into the lap of Danae of old;
For poets cherish many a strange conceit,
And love transmutes all nature by its heat.

No more the garden lessons, nor the dark
And hurried meetings in the twilight park;
But now the studious lamp, and the delights
Of firesides in the silent winter nights,
And watching from his window hour by hour
The light that burned in Princess Emma's tower.

At length one night, while musing by the fire,
O'ercome at last by his insane desire,—
For what will reckless love not do and dare?—
He crossed the court, and climbed the winding stair,
With some feigned message in the Emperor's name;
But when he to the lady's presence came
He knelt down at her feet, until she laid
Her hand upon him, like a naked blade,
And whispered in his ear: "Arise, Sir Knight,
To my heart's level, O my heart's delight."

And there he lingered till the crowing cock,
The Alectryon of the farmyard and the flock,
Sang his aubade with lusty voice and clear,
To tell the sleeping world that dawn was near.
And then they parted; but at parting, lo!
They saw the palace court-yard white with snow,
And, placid as a nun, the moon on high
Gazing from cloudy cloisters of the sky.
"Alas!" he said, "how hide the fatal line
Of footprints leading from thy door to mine,
And none returning!" Ah, he little knew
What woman's wit, when put to proof, can do!

That night the Emperor, sleepless with the cares
And troubles that attend on state affairs,
Had risen before the dawn, and musing gazed
Into the silent night, as one amazed
To see the calm that reigned o'er all supreme,

When his own reign was but a troubled dream.
The moon lit up the gables capped with snow,
And the white roofs, and half the court below,
And he beheld a form, that seemed to cower
Beneath a burden, come from Emma's tower,—
A woman, who upon her shoulders bore
Clerk Eginhard to his own private door,
And then returned in haste, but still essayed
To tread the footprints she herself had made;
And as she passed across the lighted space,
The Emperor saw his daughter Emma's face!

He started not; he did not speak or moan,
But seemed as one who hath been turned to stone;
And stood there like a statue, nor awoke
Out of his trance of pain, till morning broke,
Till the stars faded, and the moon went down,
And o'er the towers and steeples of the town
Came the gray daylight, then the sun, who took
The empire of the world with sovereign look,
Suffusing with a soft and golden glow
All the dead landscape in its shroud of snow,
Touching with flame the tapering chapel spires,
Windows and roofs, and smoke of household fires,
And kindling park and palace as he came;
The stork's nest on the chimney seemed in flame.
And thus he stood till Eginhard appeared,
Demure and modest with his comely beard
And flowing flaxen tresses, come to ask,
As was his wont, the day's appointed task.
The Emperor looked upon him with a smile,
And gently said: "My son, wait yet awhile;
This hour my council meets upon some great
And very urgent business of the state.
Come back within the hour. On thy return
The work appointed for thee shalt thou learn."

Having dismissed this gallant Troubadour,
He summoned straight his council, and secure
And steadfast in his purpose, from the throne
All the adventure of the night made known;
Then asked for sentence; and with eager breath
Some answered banishment, and others death.

Then spake the king: "Your sentence is not mine;
Life is the gift of God, and is divine;
Nor from these palace walls shall one depart
Who carries such a secret in his heart;
My better judgment points another way.
Good Alcuin, I remember how one day
When my Pepino asked you, 'What are men?'

You wrote upon his tablets with your pen,
'Guests of the grave and travellers that pass!"
This being true of all men, we, alas!
Being all fashioned of the self-same dust,
Let us be merciful as well as just;
This passing traveller, who hath stolen away
The brightest jewel of my crown to-day,
Shall of himself the precious gem restore;
By giving it, I make it mine once more.
Over those fatal footprints I will throw
My ermine mantle like another snow."

Then Eginhard was summoned to the hall,
And entered, and in presence of them all,
The Emperor said: "My son, for thou to me
Hast been a son, and evermore shalt be,
Long hast thou served thy sovereign, and thy zeal
Pleads to me with importunate appeal,
While I have been forgetful to requite
Thy service and affection as was right.

But now the hour is come, when I, thy Lord,
Will crown thy love with such supreme reward,
A gift so precious kings have striven in vain
To win it from the hands of Charlemagne."

Then sprang the portals of the chamber wide,
And Princess Emma entered, in the pride
Of birth and beauty, that in part o'ercame
The conscious terror and the blush of shame.
And the good Emperor rose up from his throne,
And taking her white hand within his own
Placed it in Eginhard's, and said: "My son,
This is the gift thy constant zeal hath won;
Thus I repay the royal debt I owe,
And cover up the footprints in the snow."

INTERLUDE

THUS ran the Student's pleasant rhyme
Of Eginhard and love and youth;
Some doubted its historic truth,
But while they doubted, ne'ertheless
Saw in it gleams of truthfulness,
And thanked the Monk of Lauresheim.

This they discussed in various mood;
Then in the silence that ensued
Was heard a sharp and sudden sound
As of a bowstring snapped in air;
And the Musician with a bound
Sprang up in terror from his chair,
And for a moment listening stood,
Then strode across the room, and found
His dear, his darling violin
Still lying safe asleep within
Its little cradle, like a child
That gives a sudden cry of pain,
And wakes to fall asleep again;
And as he looked at it and smiled,
By the uncertain light beguiled,
Despair! two strings were broken in twain.

While all lamented and made moan,
With many a sympathetic word
As if the loss had been their own,
Deeming the tones they might have heard
Sweeter than they had heard before,

They saw the Landlord at the door,
The missing man, the portly Squire!
He had not entered, but he stood
With both arms full of seasoned wood,
To feed the much-devouring fire,
That like a lion in a cage
Lashed its long tail and roared with rage.

The missing man! Ah, yes, they said,
Missing, but whither had he fled?
Where had he hidden himself away?
No farther than the barn or shed;
He had not hidden himself, nor fled;
How should he pass the rainy day
But in his barn with hens and hay,
Or mending harness, cart, or sled?
Now, having come, he needs must stay
And tell his tale as well as they.

The Landlord answered only: "These
Are logs from the dead apple-trees
Of the old orchard planted here
By the first Howe of Sudbury.
Nor oak nor maple has so clear
A flame, or burns so quietly,
Or leaves an ash so clean and white "
Thinking by this to put aside
The impending tale that terrified;
When suddenly, to his delight,
The Theologian interposed,
Saying that when the door was closed,
And they had stopped that draft of cold,
Unpleasant night air, he proposed
To tell a tale world-wide apart
From that the Student had just told ;
World-wide apart, and yet akin,

As showing that the human heart
Beats on forever as of old,
As well beneath the snow-white fold
Of Quaker kerchief, as within
Sandal or silk or cloth of gold,
And without preface would begin.

And then the clamorous clock struck eight,
Deliberate, with sonorous chime
Slow measuring out the march of time,
Like some grave Consul of old Rome
In Jupiter's temple driving home
The nails that marked the year and date.
Thus interrupted in his rhyme,
The Theologian needs must wait;

But quoted Horace, where he sings
The dire Necessity of things,
That drives into the roofs sublime
Of new-built houses of the great
The adamantine nails of Fate.

When ceased the little carillon
To herald from its wooden tower
The important transit of the hour,
The Theologian hastened on,
Content to be allowed at last
To sing his Idyl of the Past.

THE THEOLOGIAN'S TALE

ELIZABETH

I.

"Ah, how short are the days! How soon the night overtakes us!
In the old country the twilight is longer; but here in the forest
Suddenly comes the dark, with hardly a pause in its coming,
Hardly a moment between the two lights, the day and the lamplight ;
Yet how grand is the winter! How spotless the snow is, and perfect!"

Thus spake Elizabeth Haddon at nightfall to Hannah the housemaid,
As in the farm-house kitchen, that served for kitchen and parlor,
By the window she sat with her work, and looked on a landscape
White as the great white sheet that Peter saw in his vision,
By the four corners let down and descending out of the heavens.
Covered with snow were the forests of pine, and the fields and the meadows.
Nothing was dark but the sky, and the distant Delaware flowing
Down from its native hills, a peaceful and bountiful river.

Then with a smile on her lips made answer Hannah the housemaid:
"Beautiful winter! yea, the winter is beautiful, surely,
If one could only walk like a fly with one's feet on the ceiling.
But the great Delaware river is not like the Thames, as we saw it
Out of our upper windows in Rotherhithe Street in the Borough,
Crowded with masts and sails of vessels coming and going;
Here there is nothing but pines, with patches of snow on their
      branches.
There is snow in the air, and see! it is falling already;
All the roads will be blocked, and I pity Joseph to-morrow,

Breaking his way through the drifts, with his sled and oxen; and
     then, too,
How in all the world shall we get to Meeting on First-Day?"

     But Elizabeth checked her, and answered, mildly reproving:
"Surely the Lord will provide; for unto the snow he sayeth,
Be thou on the earth, the good Lord sayeth; he is it
Giveth snow like wool, like ashes scatters the hoar-frost."
So she folded her work and laid it away in her basket.

Meanwhile Hannah the housemaid had closed and fastened the
     shutters,
Spread the cloth, and lighted the lamp on the table, and placed there
Plates and cups from the dresser, the brown rye loaf, and the butter
Fresh from the dairy, and then, protecting her hand with a holder,
Took from the crane in the chimney the steaming and simmering
     kettle,
Poised it aloft in the air, and filled up the earthen teapot,
Made in Delft, and adorned with quaint and wonderful figures.

     Then Elizabeth said, "Lo! Joseph is long on his errand.
I have sent him away with a hamper of food and of clothing
For the poor in the village. A good lad and cheerful is Joseph;
In the right place is his heart, and his hand is ready and willing."

     Thus in praise of her servant she spake, and Hannah the housemaid
Laughed with her eyes, as she listened, but governed her tongue,
     and was silent,
While her mistress went on: "The house is far from the village;
We should be lonely here, were it not for Friends that in passing
Sometimes tarry o'ernight, and make us glad by their coming."

     Thereupon answered Hannah the housemaid, the thrifty, the frugal:
"Yea, they come and they tarry, as if thy house were a tavern;
Open to all are its doors, and they come and go like the pigeons

In and out of the holes of the pigeon-house over the hayloft,
Cooing and smoothing their feathers and basking themselves in the
    sunshine.

But in meekness of spirit, and calmly, Elizabeth answered:
"All I have is the Lord's, not mine to give or withhold it;
I but distribute his gifts to the poor, and to those of his people
Who in journeyings often surrender their lives to his service.
His, not mine, are the gifts, and only so far can I make them
Mine, as in giving I add my heart to whatever is given.
Therefore my excellent father first built this house in the clearing;
Though he came not himself, I came; for the Lord was my guidance,
Leading me here for this service. We must not grudge, then, to others
Ever the cup of cold water, or crumbs that fall from our table."

Thus rebuked, for a season was silent the penitent housemaid;
And Elizabeth said in tones even sweeter and softer:
"Dost thou remember, Hannah, the great MayMeeting in London,
When I was still a child, how we sat in the silent assembly,
Waiting upon the Lord in patient and passive submission?
No one spake, till at length a young man, a stranger, John Estaugh,
Moved by the Spirit, rose, as if he were John the Apostle,
Speaking such words of power that they bowed our hearts, as a
    strong wind
Bends the grass of the fields, or grain that is ripe for the sickle.
Thoughts of him to-day have been oft borne inward upon me,
Wherefore I do not know; but strong is the feeling within me
That once more I shall see a face I have never forgotten."

II.

E'en as she spake they heard the musical jangle of sleigh-bells,
First far off, with a dreamy sound and faint in the distance,
Then growing nearer and louder, and turning into the farmyard,

Till it stopped at the door, with sudden creaking of runners.
Then there were voices heard as of two men talking together,
And to herself, as she listened, upbraiding said Hannah the housemaid,
"It is Joseph come back, and I wonder what stranger is with him."

Down from its nail she took and lighted the great tin lantern
Pierced with holes, and round, and roofed like the top of a lighthouse,
And went forth to receive the coming guest at the doorway,
Casting into the dark a network of glimmer and shadow
Over the falling snow, the yellow sleigh, and the horses,
And the forms of men, snow-covered, looming gigantic.
Then giving Joseph the lantern, she entered the house with the
    stranger.
Youthful he was and tall, and his cheeks aglow with the night air;
And as he entered, Elizabeth rose, and, going to meet him,
As if an unseen power had announced and preceded his presence,
And he had come as one whose coming had long been expected,
Quietly gave him her hand, and said, "Thou art welcome, John
    Estaugh."
And the stranger replied, with staid and quiet behavior,
"Dost thou remember me still, Elizabeth? After so many
Years have passed, it seemeth a wonderful thing that I find thee.
Surely the hand of the Lord conducted me here to thy threshold.
For as I journeyed along, and pondered alone and in silence
On his ways, that are past finding out, I saw in the snow-mist,
Seemingly weary with travel, a wayfarer, who by the wayside
Paused and waited. Forthwith I remembered Queen Candace's eunuch,
How on the way that goes down from Jerusalem unto Gaza,
Reading Esaias the Prophet, he journeyed, and spake unto Philip,
Praying him to come up and sit in his chariot with him.
So I greeted the man, and he mounted the sledge beside me,
And as we talked on the way he told me of thee and thy homestead,
How, being led by the light of the Spirit, that never deceiveth,
Full of zeal for the work of the Lord, thou hadst come to this country.
And I remembered thy name, and thy father and mother in England,

And on my journey have stopped to see thee, Elizabeth Haddon,
Wishing to strengthen thy hand in the labors of love thou art doing."

And Elizabeth answered with confident voice, and serenely
Looking into his face with her innocent eyes as she answered,
"Surely the hand of the Lord is in it; his Spirit hath led thee
Out of the darkness and storm to the light and peace of my fireside."

Then, with stamping of feet, the door was opened, and Joseph
Entered, bearing the lantern, and, carefully blowing the light out,
Hung it up on its nail, and all sat down to their supper;
For underneath that roof was no distinction of persons,
But one family only, one heart, one hearth, and one household.

When the supper was ended they drew their chairs to the fireplace,
Spacious, open-hearted, profuse of flame and of firewood,
Lord of forests unfelled, and not a gleaner of fagots,
Spreading its arms to embrace with inexhaustible bounty
All who fled from the cold, exultant, laughing at winter!
Only Hannah the housemaid was busy in clearing the table,
Coming and going, and bustling about in closet and chamber.

Then Elizabeth told her story again to John Estaugh,
Going far back to the past, to the early days of her childhood;
How she had waited and watched, in all her doubts and besetments
Comforted with the extendings and holy, sweet inflowings
Of the spirit of love, till the voice imperative sounded,
And she obeyed the voice, and cast in her lot with her people
Here in the desert land, and God would provide for the issue.

Meanwhile Joseph sat with folded hands, and demurely
Listened, or seemed to listen, and in the silence that followed
Nothing was heard for a while but the step of Hannah the housemaid
Walking the floor overhead, and setting the chambers in order.
And Elizabeth said, with a smile of compassion, "The maiden

Hath a light heart in her breast, but her feet are heavy and awkward."
Inwardly Joseph laughed, but governed his tongue, and was silent.

Then came the hour of sleep, death's counterfeit, nightly rehearsal
Of the great Silent Assembly, the Meeting of shadows, where no man
Speaketh, but all are still, and the peace and rest are unbroken!
Silently over that house the blessing of slumber descended.
But when the morning dawned, and the sun uprose in his splendor,
Breaking his way through clouds that encumbered his path in the
       heavens,
Joseph was seen with his sled and oxen breaking a pathway
Through the drifts of snow; the horses already were harnessed,
And John Estaugh was standing and taking leave at the threshold,
Saying that he should return at the Meeting in May; while above them
Hannah the housemaid, the homely, was looking out of the attic,
Laughing aloud at Joseph, then suddenly closing the casement,
As the bird in a cuckoo-clock peeps out of its window,
Then disappears again, and closes the shutter behind it.

III.

Now was the winter gone, and the snow; and Robin the Redbreast,
Boasted on bush and tree it was he, it was he and no other
That had covered with leaves the Babes in the Wood, and blithely
All the birds sang with him, and little cared for his boasting,
Little cared for his Babes in the Wood, or the Cruel Uncle, and only
Sang for the mates they had chosen, and cared for the nests they
       were building.
With them, but more sedately and meekly, Elizabeth Haddon
Sang in her inmost heart, but her lips were silent and songless.
Thus came the lovely spring with a rush of blossoms and music,
Flooding the earth with flowers, and the air with melodies vernal.

Then it came to pass, one pleasant morning, that slowly
Up the road there came a cavalcade, as of pilgrims,

Men and women, wending their way to the Quarterly Meeting
In the neighboring town; and with them came riding John Estaugh.
At Elizabeth's door they stopped to rest, and alighting
Tasted the currant wine, and the bread of rye, and the honey
Brought from the hives, that stood by the sunny wall of the garden;
Then remounted their horses, refreshed, and continued their journey,
And Elizabeth with them, and Joseph, and Hannah the housemaid.
But, as they started, Elizabeth lingered a little, and leaning
Over her horse's neck, in a whisper said to John Estaugh:
"Tarry awhile behind, for I have something to tell thee,
Not to be spoken lightly, nor in the presence of others;
Them it concerneth not, only thee and me it concerneth."
And they rode slowly along through the woods, conversing together.
It was a pleasure to breathe the fragrant air of the forest;
It was a pleasure to live on that bright and happy May morning!

    Then Elizabeth said, though still with a certain reluctance,
As if impelled to reveal a secret she fain would have guarded:
"I will no longer conceal what is laid upon me to tell thee;
I have received from the Lord a charge to love thee, John Estaugh."

    And John Estaugh made answer, surprised by the words she had
        spoken,
"Pleasant to me are thy converse, thy ways, thy meekness of spirit;
Pleasant thy frankness of speech, and thy soul's immaculate whiteness,
Love without dissimulation, a holy and inward adorning.
But I have yet no light to lead me, no voice to direct me.
When the Lord's work is done, and the toil and the labor completed
He hath appointed to me, I will gather into the stillness
Of my own heart awhile, and listen and wait for his guidance."

    Then Elizabeth said, not troubled nor wounded in spirit,
"So is it best, John Estaugh. We will not speak of it further.
It hath been laid upon me to tell thee this, for to-morrow
Thou art going away, across the sea, and I know not

When I shall see thee more; but if the Lord hath decreed it,
Thou wilt return again to seek me here and to find me."
And they rode onward in silence, and entered the town with the others.

IV.

Ships that pass in the night, and speak each other in passing,
Only a signal shown and a distant voice in the darkness;
So on the ocean of life we pass and speak one another,
Only a look and a voice, then darkness again and a silence.

Now went on as of old the quiet life of the homestead.
Patient and unrepining Elizabeth labored, in all things
Mindful not of herself, but bearing the burdens of others,
Always thoughtful and kind and untroubled; and Hannah the
          housemaid
Diligent early and late, and rosy with washing and scouring,
Still as of old disparaged the eminent merits of Joseph,
And was at times reproved for her light and frothy behavior,
For her shy looks, and her careless words, and her evil surmisings,
Being pressed down somewhat, like a cart with sheaves overladen,
As she would sometimes say to Joseph, quoting the Scriptures.

Meanwhile John Estaugh departed across the sea, and departing
Carried hid in his heart a secret sacred and precious,
Filling its chambers with fragrance, and seeming to him in its
          sweetness
Mary's ointment of spikenard, that filled all the house with its odor.
O lost days of delight, that are wasted in doubting and waiting!
O lost hours and days in which we might have been happy!
But the light shone at last, and guided his wavering footsteps,
And at last came the voice, imperative, questionless, certain.

Then John Estaugh came back o'er the sea for the gift that was
    offered,
Better than houses and lands, the gift of a woman's affection.
And on the First-Day that followed, he rose in the Silent Assembly,
Holding in his strong hand a hand that trembled a little,
Promising to be kind and true and faithful in all things.
Such were the marriage-rites of John and Elizabeth Estaugh.

And not otherwise Joseph, the honest, the diligent servant,
Sped in his bashful wooing with homely Hannah, the housemaid;
For when he asked her the question, she answered, "Nay"; and then
    added:
"But thee may make believe, and see what will come of it, Joseph."

INTERLUDE

"A PLEASANT and a winsome tale,"
The Student said, "though somewhat pale
And quiet in its coloring,
As if it caught its tone and air
From the gray suits that Quakers wear;
Yet worthy of some German bard,
Hebel, or Voss, or Eberhard,
Who love of humble themes to sing,
In humble verse; but no more true
Than was the tale I told to you."

The Theologian made reply,
And with some warmth, "That I deny;
'Tis no invention of my own,
But something well and widely known
To readers of a riper age,
Writ by the skilful hand that wrote
The Indian tale of Hobomok,
And Philothea's classic page.
I found it like a waif afloat,
Or dulse uprooted from its rock,
On the swift tides that ebb and flow
In daily papers, and at flood
Bear freighted vessels to and fro,
But later, when the ebb is low,
Leave a long waste of sand and mud."

"It matters little," quoth the Jew;
"The cloak of truth is lined with lies,
Sayeth some proverb old and wise;
And Love is master of all arts,
And puts it into human hearts
The strangest things to say and do."
And here the controversy closed
Abruptly, ere 't was well begun;
For the Sicilian interposed
With, "Lordlings, listen, every one
That listen may, unto a tale
That's merrier than the nightingale;
A tale that cannot boast, forsooth,
A single rag or shred of truth;
That does not leave the mind in doubt
As to the with it or without;
A naked falsehood and absurd
As mortal ever told or heard.
Therefore I tell it; or, maybe,
Simply because it pleases me."

THE SICILIAN'S TALE

THE MONK OF CASAL-MAGGIORE.

ONCE on a time, some centuries ago,
    In the hot sunshine two Franciscan friars
Wended their weary way with footsteps slow
    Back to their convent, whose white walls and spires
Gleamed on the hillside like a patch of snow;
    Covered with dust they were, and torn by briers,
And bore like sumpter-mules upon their backs
The badge of poverty, their beggar's sacks.

The first was Brother Anthony, a spare
    And silent man, with pallid cheeks and thin,
Much given to vigils, penance, fasting, prayer,
    Solemn and gray, and worn with discipline,
As if his body but white ashes were,
    Heaped on the living coals that glowed within;
A simple monk, like many of his day,
Whose instinct was to listen and obey.

A different man was Brother Timothy,
    Of larger mould and of a coarser paste;
A rubicund and stalwart monk was he,
    Broad in the shoulders, broader in the waist.
Who often filled the dull refectory
    With noise by which the convent was disgraced,
But to the mass-book gave but little heed,
By reason he had never learned to read.

Now, as they passed the outskirts of a wood,
    They saw, with mingled pleasure and surprise,
Fast tethered to a tree an ass, that stood
    Lazily winking his large, limpid eyes.
The farmer Gilbert of that neighborhood
    His owner was, who, looking for supplies
Of fagots, deeper in the wood had strayed,
Leaving his beast to ponder in the shade.

As soon as Brother Timothy espied
    The patient animal, he said: "Good-lack!
Thus for our needs doth Providence provide;
    We'll lay our wallets on the creature's back."
This being done, he leisurely untied
    From head and neck the halter of the jack,
And put it round his own, and to the tree
Stood tethered fast as if the ass were he.

And, bursting forth into a merry laugh,
    He cried to Brother Anthony: "Away!
And drive the ass before you with your staff;
    And when you reach the convent you may say
You left me at a farm, half tired and half
    Ill with a fever, for a night and day,
And that the farmer lent this ass to bear
Our wallets, that are heavy with good fare."

Now Brother Anthony, who knew the pranks
    Of Brother Timothy, would not persuade
Or reason with him on his quirks and cranks,
    But, being obedient, silently obeyed ;
And, smiting with his staff the ass's flanks,
    Drove him before him over hill and glade,
Safe with his provend to the convent gate,
Leaving poor Brother Timothy to his fate.

Then Gilbert, laden with fagots for his fire,
    Forth issued from the wood, and stood aghast
To see the ponderous body of the friar
    Standing where he had left his donkey last.
Trembling he stood, and dared not venture nigher,
    But stared, and gaped, and crossed himself full fast;
For, being credulous and of little wit,
He thought it was some demon from the pit.

While speechless and bewildered thus he gazed,
    And dropped his load of fagots on the ground,
Quoth Brother Timothy: "Be not amazed
    That where you left a donkey should be found
A poor Franciscan friar, half-starved and crazed,
    Standing demure and with a halter bound;
But set me free, and hear the piteous story
Of Brother Timothy of Casal-Maggiore.

"I am a sinful man, although you see
    I wear the consecrated cowl and cape;
You never owned an ass, but you owned me,
    Changed and transformed from my own natural shape
All for the deadly sin of gluttony,
    From which I could not otherwise escape,
Than by this penance, dieting on grass,
And being worked and beaten as an ass.

"Think of the ignominy I endured;
    Think of the miserable life I led,
The toil and blows to which I was inured,
    My wretched lodging in a windy shed,
My scanty fare so grudgingly procured,
    The damp and musty straw that formed my bed!
But, having done this penance for my sins,
My life as man and monk again begins."

The simple Gilbert, hearing words like these,
    Was conscience-stricken, and fell down apace
Before the friar upon his bended knees,
    And with a suppliant voice implored his grace;
And the good monk, now very much at ease,
    Granted him pardon with a smiling face,
Nor could refuse to be that night his guest,
It being late, and he in need of rest.

Upon a hillside, where the olive thrives,
    With figures painted on its whitewashed walls,
The cottage stood; and near the humming hives
    Made murmurs as of far-off waterfalls;
A place where those who love secluded lives
    Might live content, and, free from noise and brawls,
Like Claudian's Old Man of Verona here
Measure by fruits the slow-revolving year.

And, coming to this cottage of content,
    They found his children, and the buxom wench
His wife, Dame Cicely, and his father, bent
    With years and labor, seated on a bench,
Repeating over some obscure event
    In the old wars of Milanese and French;
All welcomed the Franciscan, with a sense
Of sacred awe and humble reverence.

When Gilbert told them what had come to pass,
    How beyond question, cavil, or surmise,
Good Brother Timothy had been their ass,
    You should have seen the wonder in their eyes;
You should have heard them cry," Alas! alas!"
    Have heard their lamentations and their sighs!
For all believed the story, and began
To see a saint in this afflicted man.

Forthwith there was prepared a grand repast,
    To satisfy the craving of the friar
After so rigid and prolonged a fast
    The bustling housewife stirred the kitchen fire;
Then her two favorite pullets and her last
    Were put to death, at her express desire,
And served up with a salad in a bowl,
And flasks of country wine to crown the whole.

It would not be believed should I repeat
    How hungry Brother Timothy appeared;
It was a pleasure but to see him eat,
    His white teeth flashing through his russet beard,
His face aglow and flushed with wine and meat,
    His roguish eyes that rolled and laughed and leered!
Lord! how he drank the blood-red country wine.
As if the village vintage were divine!

And all the while he talked without surcease,
    And told his merry tales with jovial glee
That never flagged, but rather did increase,
    And laughed aloud as if insane were he,
And wagged his red beard, matted like a fleece,
    And cast such glances at Dame Cicely
That Gilbert now grew angry with his guest,
And thus in words his rising wrath expressed.

"Good father," said he, "easily we see
    How needful in some persons, and how right,
Mortification of the flesh may be.
    The indulgence you have given it to-night,
After long penance, clearly proves to me
    Your strength against temptation is but slight,
And shows the dreadful peril you are in
Of a relapse into your deadly sin.

"To-morrow morning, with the rising sun,
    Go back unto your convent, nor refrain
From fasting and from scourging, for you run
    Great danger to become an ass again,
Since monkish flesh and asinine are one;
    Therefore be wise, nor longer here remain,
Unless you wish the scourge should be applied
By other hands, that will not spare your hide."

When this the monk had heard, his color fled
    And then returned, like lightning in the air,
Till he was all one blush from foot to head,
    And even the bald spot in his russet hair
Turned from its usual pallor to bright red!
    The old man was asleep upon his chair.
Then all retired, and sank into the deep
And helpless imbecility of sleep.

They slept until the dawn of day drew near,
    Till the cock should have crowed, but did not crow,
For they had slain the shining chanticleer
    And eaten him for supper, as you know.
The monk was up betimes and of good cheer,
    And, having breakfasted, made haste to go,
As if he heard the distant matin bell,
And had but little time to say farewell.

Fresh was the morning as the breath of kine;
    Odors of herbs commingled with the sweet
Balsamic exhalations of the pine;
    A haze was in the air presaging heat;
Uprose the sun above the Appenine,
    And all the misty valleys at its feet.
Were full of the delirious song of birds,
Voices of men, and bells, and low of herds.

All this to Brother Timothy was naught;
    He did not care for scenery, nor here
His busy fancy found the thing it sought;
    But when he saw the convent walls appear,
And smoke from kitchen chimneys upward caught
    And whirled aloft into the atmosphere,
He quickened his slow footsteps, like a beast
That scents the stable a league off at least.

And as he entered through the convent gate
    He saw there in the court the ass, who stood
Twirling his ears about, and seemed to wait,
    Just as he found him waiting in the wood;
And told the Prior that, to alleviate
    The daily labors of the brotherhood,
The owner, being a man of means and thrift,
Bestowed him on the convent as a gift.

And thereupon the Prior for many days
    Revolved this serious matter in his mind,
And turned it over many different ways,
    Hoping that some safe issue he might find;
But stood in fear of what the world would say,
    If he accepted presents of this kind,
Employing beasts of burden for the packs
That lazy monks should carry on their backs.

Then, to avoid all scandal of the sort,
    And stop the mouth of cavil, he decreed
That he would cut the tedious matter short,
    And sell the ass with all convenient speed,
Thus saving the expense of his support,
    And hoarding something for a time of need.
So he despatched him to the neighboring Fair,
And freed himself from cumber and from care.

It happened now by chance, as some might say,
    Others perhaps would call it destiny,
Gilbert was at the Fair; and heard a bray,
    And nearer came, and saw that it was he,
And whispered in his ear, "Ah, lackaday!
    Good father, the rebellious flesh, I see,
Has changed you back into an ass again,
And all my admonitions were in vain."

The ass, who felt this breathing in his ear,
    Did not turn round to look, but shook his head,
As if he were not pleased these words to hear,
    And contradicted all that had been said.
And this made Gilbert cry in voice more clear,
    "I know you well; your hair is russet-red;
Do not deny it; for you are the same
Franciscan friar, and Timothy by name."

The ass, though now the secret had come out,
    Was obstinate, and shook his head again;
Until a crowd was gathered round about.
    To hear this dialogue between the twain;
And raised their voices in a noisy shout
    When Gilbert tried to make the matter plain,
And flouted him and mocked him all day long
With laughter and with jibes and scraps of song.

"If this be Brother Timothy," they cried,
    "Buy him, and feed him on the tenderest grass;
Thou canst not do too much for one so tried
    As to be twice transformed into an ass."
So simple Gilbert bought him, and untied
    His halter, and o'er mountain and morass
He led him homeward, talking as he went
Of good behavior and a mind content.

The children saw them coming, and advanced,
    Shouting with joy, and hung about his neck,—
Not Gilbert's, but the ass's, —round him danced,
    And wove green garlands wherewithal to deck
His sacred person; for again it chanced
    Their childish feelings, without rein or check,
Could not discriminate in any way
A donkey from a friar of Orders Gray.

"O Brother Timothy," the children said,
    "You have come back to us just as before;
We were afraid, and thought that you were dead,
    And we should never see you any more."
And then they kissed the white star on his head,
    That like a birth-mark or a badge he wore,
And patted him upon the neck and face,
And said a thousand things with childish grace.

Thenceforward and forever he was known
    As Brother Timothy, and led alway
A life of luxury, till he had grown
    Ungrateful, being stuffed with corn and hay,
And very vicious. Then in angry tone,
    Rousing himself, poor Gilbert said one day,
"When simple kindness is misunderstood
A little flagellation may do good."

His many vices need not here be told;
    Among them was a habit that he had
Of flinging up his heels at young and old,
    Breaking his halter, running off like mal
O'er pasture-lands and meadow, wood and wold,
    And other misdemeanors quite as bad;
But worst of all was breaking from his shed
At night, and ravaging the cabbage-bed.

So Brother Timothy went back once more
    To his old life of labor and distress;
Was beaten worse than he had been before;
    And now, instead of comfort and caress,
Came labors manifold and trials sore;
    And as his toils increased his food grew less,
Until at last the great consoler, Death,
Ended his many sufferings with his breath.

Great was the lamentation when he died;
    And mainly that he died impenitent;
Dame Cicely bewailed, the children cried,
    The old man still remembered the event
In the French war, and Gilbert magnified
    His many virtues, as he came and went,
And said: "Heaven pardon Brother Timothy,
And keep us from the sin of gluttony."

INTERLUDE

"SIGNOR LUIGI," said the Jew,
When the Sicilian's tale was told,
"The were-wolf is a legend old,
But the were-ass is something new,
And yet for one I think it true.
The days of wonder have not ceased;
If there are beasts in forms of men,
As sure it happens now and then,
Why may not man become a beast,
In way of punishment at least?

"But this I will not now discuss;
I leave the theme, that we may thus
Remain within the realm of song.
The story that I told before,
Though not acceptable to all,
At least you did not find too long.
I beg you, let me try again,
With something in a different vein,
Before you bid the curtain fall.
Meanwhile keep watch upon the door,
Nor let the Landlord leave his chair,
Lest he should vanish into air,
And thus elude our search once more."

Thus saying, from his lips he blew
A little cloud of perfumed breath,
And then, as if it were a clew
To lead his footsteps safely through,
Began his tale as followeth.

THE SPANISH JEW'S SECOND TALE

SCANDERBEG.

THE battle is fought and won
By King Ladislaus the Hun,
In fire of hell and death's frost,
On the day of Pentecost.
And in rout before his path
From the field of battle red
Flee all that are not dead
Of the army of Amurath.

In the darkness of the night
Iskander, the pride and boast
Of that mighty Othman host,
With his routed Turks, takes flight
From the battle fought and lost
On the day of Pentecost;
Leaving behind him dead
The army of Amurath,
The vanguard as it led,
The rearguard as it fled,
Mown down in the bloody swath
Of the battle's aftermath.

But he cared not for Hospodars,
Nor for Baron or Voivode,
As on through the night he rode
And gazed at the fateful stars,
That were shining overhead;
But smote his steed with his staff,
And smiled to himself, and said:
"This is the time to laugh."

In the middle of the night,
In a halt of the hurrying flight,
There came a Scribe of the King
Wearing his signet ring,
And said in a voice severe :
"This is the first dark blot
On thy name, George Castriot!
Alas! why art thou here,
And the army of Amurath slain,
And left on the battle plain?"

And Iskander answered and said:
"They lie on the bloody sod
By the hoofs of horses trod;
But this was the decree
Of the watchers overhead;
For the war belongeth to God,
And in battle who are we,
Who are we, that shall withstand
The wind of his lifted hand?"

Then he bade them bind with chains
This man of books and brains;
And the Scribe said: "What misdeed
Have I done, that without need,
Thou doest to me this thing?"
And Iskander answering
Said unto him: "Not one
Misdeed to me hast thou done;
But for fear that thou shouldst run
And hide thyself from me,
Have I done this unto thee.

"Now write me a writing, O Scribe,
And a blessing be on thy tribe!
A writing sealed with thy ring,
To King Amurath's Pasha
In the city of Croia,
The city moated and walled,
That he surrender the same
In the name of my master, the King;
For what is writ in his name
Can never be recalled."

And the Scribe bowed low in dread,
And unto Iskander said:
"Allah is great and just,
But we are as ashes and dust;
How shall I do this thing,
When I know that my guilty head
Will be forfeit to the King?"

Then swift as a shooting star
The curved and shining blade
Of Iskander's scimetar
From its sheath, with jewels bright,
Shot, as he thundered: "Write!"
And the trembling Scribe obeyed,
And wrote in the fitful glare
Of the bivouac fire apart,
With the chill of the midnight air
On his forehead white and bare,
And the chill of death in his heart.

Then again Iskander cried:
"Now follow whither I ride,
For here thou must not stay.
Thou shalt be as my dearest friend,

And honors without end
Shall surround thee on every side,
And attend thee night and day."
But the sullen Scribe replied:
"Our pathways here divide;
Mine leadeth not thy way."

And even as he spoke
Fell a sudden scimetar stroke,
When no one else was near;
And the Scribe sank to the ground,
As a stone, pushed from the brink
Of a black pool, might sink
With a sob and disappear;
And no one saw the deed;
And in the stillness around
No sound was heard but the sound
Of the hoofs of Iskander's steed,
As forward he sprang with a bound.

Then onward he rode and afar,
With scarce three hundred men,
Through river and forest and fen,
O'er the mountains of Argentar;
And his heart was merry within,
When he crossed the river Drin,
And saw in the gleam of the morn
The White Castle Ak-Hissar,
The city Croia called,
The city moated and walled,
The city where he was born,—
And above it the morning star.

Then his trumpeters in the van
On their silver bugles blew,
And in crowds about him ran

Albanian and Turkoman,
That the sound together drew.
And he feasted with his friends,
And when they were warm with wine,
He said: "O friends of mine,
Behold what fortune sends,
And what the fates design!
King Amurath commands
That my father's wide domain,
This city and all its lands,
Shall be given to me again."

Then to the Castle White
He rode in regal state,
And entered in at the gate
In all his arms bedight,
And gave to the Pasha
Who ruled in Croia
The writing of the King,
Sealed with his signet ring.

And the Pasha bowed his head,
And after a silence said :
"Allah is just and great!
I yield to the will divine,
The city and lands are thine;
Who shall contend with fate?"

Anon from the castle walls
The crescent banner falls,
And the crowd beholds instead,
Like a portent in the sky,
Iskander's banner fly,
The Black Eagle with double head;
And a shout ascends on high,

For men's souls are tired of the Turks,
And their wicked ways and works,
That have made of Ak-Hissar
A city of the plague;
And the loud, exultant cry
That echoes wide and far
Is: "Long live Scanderbeg!"

It was thus Iskander came
Once more unto his own;
And the tidings, like the flame
Of a conflagration blown
By the winds of summer, ran,
Till the land was in a blaze,
And the cities far and near,
Sayeth Ben Joshua Ben Meir,
In his Book of the Words of the Days,
"Were taken as a man
Would take the tip of his ear."

INTERLUDE

"Now that is after my own heart,"
The Poet cried; "one understands
Your swarthy hero Scanderbeg,
Gauntlet on hand and boot on leg,
And skilled in every warlike art,
Riding through his Albanian lands,
And following the auspicious star
That shone for him o'er Ak-Hissar."

The Theologian added here
His word of praise not less sincere,
Although he ended with a jibe;
"The hero of romance and song
Was born," he said, "to right the wrong;
And I approve; but all the same
That bit of treason with the Scribe
Adds nothing to your hero's fame."

The Student praised the good old times,
And liked the canter of the rhymes,
That had a hoofbeat in their sound;
But longed some further word to hear
Of the old chronicler Ben Meir,
And where his volume might be found.
The tall Musician walked the room
With folded arms and gleaming eyes,
As if he saw the Vikings rise,
Gigantic shadows in the gloom;
And much he talked of their emprise,

And meteors seen in Northern skies,
And Heimdal's horn, and day of doom.
But the Sicilian laughed again ;
"This is the time to laugh," he said,
For the whole story he well knew
Was an invention of the Jew,
Spun from the cobwebs in his brain,
And of the same bright scarlet thread
As was the Tale of Kambalu.

Only the Landlord spake no word;
'T was doubtful whether he had heard
The tale at all, so full of care
Was he of his impending fate,
That, like the sword of Damocles,
Above his head hung blank and bare,
Suspended by a single hair,
So that he could not sit at case,
But sighed and looked disconsolate,
And shifted restless in his chair,
Revolving how he might evade
The blow of the descending blade.

The Student came to his relief
By saying in his easy way
To the Musician: "Calm your grief,
My fair Apollo of the North,
Balder the Beautiful and so forth;
Although your magic lyre or lute
With broken strings is lying mute,
Still you can tell some doleful tale
Of shipwreck in a midnight gale,
Or something of the kind to suit
The mood that we are in to-night
For what is marvellous and strange;

So give your nimble fancy range,
And we will follow in its flight."

But the Musician shook his head;
"No tale I tell to-night," he said,
"While my poor instrument lies there,
Even as a child with vacant stare
Lies in its little coffin dead."

Yet, being urged, he said at last :
"There comes to me out of the Past
A voice, whose tones are sweet and wild,
Singing a song almost divine,
And with a tear in every line;
An ancient ballad, that my nurse
Sang to me when I was a child,
In accents tender as the verse;
And sometimes wept, and sometimes smiled
While singing it, to see arise
The look of wonder in my eyes,
And feel my heart with terror beat.
This simple ballad I retain
Clearly imprinted on my brain,
And as a tale will now repeat."

THE MUSICIAN'S TALE

The Mother's Ghost

SVEND DYRING he rideth adown the glade;
   I myself was young!
There he hath wooed him so winsome a maid;
   Fair words gladden so many a heart.

Together were they for seven years,
And together children six were theirs.

Then came Death abroad through the land,
And blighted the beautiful lily-wand.

Svend Dyring he rideth adown the glade,
And again hath he wooed him another maid.

He hath wooed him a maid and brought home a bride,
But she was bitter and full of pride.

When she came driving into the yard,
There stood the six children weeping so hard.

There stood the small children with sorrowful heart;
From before her feet she thrust them apart.

She gave to them neither ale nor bread;
"Ye shall suffer hunger and hate," she said.

She took from them their quilts of blue,
And said: "Ye shall lie on the straw we strew."

She took from them the great waxlight;
"Now ye shall lie in the dark at night."

In the evening late they cried with cold;
The mother heard it under the mould.

The woman heard it the earth below:
"To my little children I must go."

She standeth before the Lord of all:
"And may I go to my children small?"

She prayed him so long, and would not cease,
Until he bade her depart in peace.

"At cock-crow thou shalt return again;
Longer thou shalt not there remain!"

She girded up her sorrowful bones,
And rifted the walls and the marble stones.

As through the village she flitted by,
The watch-dogs howled aloud to the sky.

When she came to the castle gate,
There stood her eldest daughter in wait.

"Why standest thou here, dear daughter mine?
How fares it with brothers and sisters thine?"

"Never art thou mother of mine,
For my mother was both fair and fine.

"My mother was white, with checks of red,
But thou art pale, and like to the dead."

"How should I be fair and fine?
I have been dead; pale checks are mine.

"How should I be white and red,
So long, so long have I been dead?

When she came in at the chamber door,
There stood the small children weeping sore.

One she braided, another she brushed,
The third she lifted, the fourth she hushed.

The fifth she took on her lap and pressed,
As if she would suckle it at her breast.

Then to her eldest daughter said she,
"Do thou bid Svend Dyring come hither to me."

Into the chamber when he came
She spake to him in anger and shame.

"I left behind me both ale and bread;
My children hunger and are not fed.

"I left behind me quilts of blue;
My children lie on the straw ye strew.

"I left behind me the great waxlight;
My children lie in the dark at night.

"If I come again unto your hall,
As cruel a fate shall you befall!

"Now crows the cock with feathers red;
Back to the earth must all the dead.

"Now crows the cock with feathers swart;
The gates of heaven fly wide apart.

"Now crows the cock with feathers white;
I can abide no longer to-night."

Whenever they heard the watch-dogs wail,
They gave the children bread and ale.

Whenever they heard the watch-dogs bay,
They feared lest the dead were on their way.

Whenever they heard the watch-dogs bark;
   I myself was young!
They feared the dead out there in the dark.
   Fair words gladden so many a heart.

INTERLUDE

TOUCHED by the pathos of these rhymes,
The Theologian said: "All praise
Be to the ballads of old times
And to the bards of simple ways,
Who walked with Nature hand in hand,
Whose country was their Holy Land,
Whose singing robes were homespun brown
From looms of their own native town,
Which they were not ashamed to wear,
And not of silk or sendal gay,
Nor decked with fanciful array
Of cockle-shells from Outre-Mer."

To whom the student answered: "Yes;
All praise and honor! I confess
That bread and ale, home-baked, home-brewed,
Are wholesome and nutritious food,
But not enough for all our needs;
Poets—the best of them—are birds
Of passage; where their instinct leads
They range abroad for thoughts and words,
And from all climes bring home the seeds
That germinate in flowers or weeds.
They are not fowls in barnyards born
To cackle o'er a grain of corn;
And, if you shut the horizon down
To the small limits of their town,
What do you but degrade your bard
Till he at last becomes as one

Who thinks the all-encircling sun
Rises and sets in his back yard?"

The Theologian said again:
"It may be so; yet I maintain
That what is native still is best,
And little care I for the rest.
'T is a long story; time would fail
To tell it, and the hour is late;
We will not waste it in debate,
But listen to our Landlord's tale."

And thus the sword of Damocles
Descending not by slow degrees,
But suddenly, on the Landlord fell,
Who blushing, and with much demur
And many vain apologies,
Plucking up heart, began to tell
The Rhyme of one Sir Christopher.

THE LANDLORD'S TALE

THE RHYME OF SIR CHRISTOPHER

It was Sir Christopher Gardiner,
Knight of the Holy Sepulchre,
From Merry England over the sea,
Who stepped upon this continent
As if his august presence lent
A glory to the colony.

You should have seen him in the street
Of the little Boston of Winthrop's time,
His rapier dangling at his feet,
Doublet and hose and boots complete,
Prince Rupert hat with ostrich plume,
Gloves that exhaled a faint perfume,
Luxuriant curls and air sublime,
And superior manners now obsolete!

He had a way of saying things
That made one think of courts and kings,
And lords and ladies of high degree;
So that not having been at court
Seemed something very little short
Of treason or lese-majesty,
Such an accomplished knight was he.

His dwelling was just beyond the town,
At what he called his country-seat;
For, careless of Fortune's smile or frown,
And weary grown of the world and its ways,
He wished to pass the rest of his days
In a private life and a calm retreat.

But a double life was the life he led,
And, while professing to be in search
Of a godly course, and willing, he said,
Nay, anxious to join the Puritan church,
He made of all this but small account,
And passed his idle hours instead
With roystering Morton of Merry Mount,
That pettifogger from Furnival's Inn,
Lord of misrule and riot and sin,
Who looked on the wine when it was red.

This country-seat was little more
Than a cabin of logs; but in front of the door
A modest flower-bed thickly sown
With sweet alyssum and columbine
Made those who saw it at once divine
The touch of some other hand than his own.
And first it was whispered, and then it was known,
That he in secret was harboring there
A little lady with golden hair,
Whom he called his cousin, but whom he had wed
In the Italian manner, as men said,
And great was the scandal everywhere.

But worse than this was the vague surmise,
Though none could vouch for it or aver,
That the Knight of the Holy Sepulchre
Was only a Papist in disguise;
And the more to embitter their bitter lives,
And the more to trouble the public mind,
Came letters from England, from two other wives,
Whom he had carelessly left behind;
Both of them letters of such a kind
As made the governor hold his breath;
The one imploring him straight to send

The husband home, that he might amend;
The other asking his instant death,
As the only way to make an end.

The wary governor deemed it right,
When all this wickedness was revealed,
To send his warrant signed and sealed,
And take the body of the knight.
Armed with this mighty instrument,
The marshal, mounting his gallant steed,
Rode forth from town at the top of his speed,
And followed by all his bailiffs bold,
As if on high achievement bent,
To storm some castle or stronghold,
Challenge the warders on the wall,
And seize in his ancestral hall
A robber-baron grim and old.

But when through all the dust and heat
He came to Sir Christopher's country-scat,
No knight he found, nor warder there,
But the little lady with golden hair,
Who was gathering in the bright sunshine
The sweet alyssum and columbine;
While gallant Sir Christopher, all so gay,
Being forewarned, through the postern gate
Of his castle wall had tripped away,
And was keeping a little holiday
In the forests, that bounded his estate.

Then as a trusty squire and true
The marshal searched the castle through,
Not crediting what the lady said;
Searched from cellar to garret in vain,
And, finding no knight, came out again

And arrested the golden damsel instead,
And bore her in triumph into the town,
While from her eyes the tears rolled down
On the sweet alyssum and columbine,
That she held in her fingers white and fine.

The governor's heart was moved to see
So fair a creature caught within
The snares of Satan and of sin,
And read her a little homily
On the folly and wickedness of the lives
Of women, half cousins and half wives;
But, seeing that naught his words availed,
He sent her away in a ship that sailed
For Merry England over the sea,
To the other two wives in the old countree,
To search her further, since he had failed
To come at the heart of the mystery.

Meanwhile Sir Christopher wandered away
Through pathless woods for a month and a day,
Shooting pigeons, and sleeping at night
With the noble savage, who took delight
In his feathered hat and his velvet vest.
His gun and his rapier and the rest.
But as soon as the noble savage heard
That a bounty was offered for this gay bird,
He wanted to slay him out of hand,
And bring in his beautiful scalp for a show,
Like the glossy head of a kite or crow,
Until he was made to understand
They wanted the bird alive, not dead;
Then he followed him whithersoever he fled,
Through forest and field, and hunted him down,
And brought him prisoner into the town.

Alas! it was a rueful sight,
To see this melancholy knight
In such a dismal and hapless case;
His hat deformed by stain and dent,
His plumage broken, his doublet rent,
His beard and flowing locks forlorn,
Matted, dishevelled, and unshorn,
His boots with dust and mire besprent;
But dignified in his disgrace,
And wearing an unblushing face.
And thus before the magistrate
He stood to hear the doom of fate.
In vain he strove with wonted ease
To modify and extenuate
His evil deeds in church and state,
For gone was now his power to please;
And his pompous words had no more weight
Than feathers flying in the breeze.

With suavity equal to his own
The governor lent a patient ear
To the speech evasive and highflown,
In which he endeavored to make clear
That colonial laws were too severe
When applied to a gallant cavalier,
A gentleman born, and so well known,
And accustomed to move in a higher sphere.

All this the Puritan governor heard,
And deigned in answer never a word;
But in summary manner shipped away
In a vessel that sailed from Salem bay,
This splendid and famous cavalier,
With his Rupert hat and his popery,
To Merry England over the sea,
As being unmeet to inhabit here.

Thus endeth the Rhyme of Sir Christopher,
Knight of the Holy Sepulchre,
The first who furnished this barren land
With apples of Sodom and ropes of sand.

FINALE

THESE are the tales those merry guests
Told to each other, well or ill;
Like summer birds that lift their crests
Above the borders of their nests
And twitter, and again are still.

These are the tales, or new or old,
In idle moments idly told;
Flowers of the field with petals thin,
Lilies that neither toil nor spin,
And tufts of wayside weeds and gorse
Hung in the parlor of the inn
Beneath the sign of the Red Horse.

And still, reluctant to retire,
The friends sat talking by the fire
And watched the smouldering embers burn.
To ashes, and flash up again
Into a momentary glow,
Lingering like them when forced to go,
And going when they would remain;
For on the morrow they must turn
Their faces homeward, and the pain
Of parting touched with its unrest
A tender nerve in every breast.

But sleep at last the victory won;
They must be stirring with the sun,
And drowsily good night they said,
And went still gossiping to bed,
And left the parlor wrapped in gloom.
The only live thing in the room
Was the old clock, that in its pace
Kept time with the revolving spheres
And constellations in their flight,
And struck with its uplifted mace
The dark, unconscious hours of night,
To senseless and unlistening ears.

Uprose the sun; and every guest,
Uprisen, was soon equipped and dressed
For journeying home and city-ward;
The old stage-coach was at the door,
With horses harnessed, long before
The sunshine reached the withered sward
Beneath the oaks, whose branches hoar
Murmured: "Farewell forevermore."

"Farewell!" the portly Landlord cried;
"Farewell!" the parting guests replied,
But little thought that nevermore
Their feet would pass that threshold o'er;
That nevermore together there
Would they assemble, free from care,
To hear the oaks' mysterious roar,
And breathe the wholesome country air.

Where are they now? What lands and skies
Paint pictures in their friendly eyes?
What hope deludes, what promise cheers,
What pleasant voices fill their ears?
Two are beyond the salt sea waves,

And three already in their graves.
Perchance the living still may look
Into the pages of this book,
And see the days of long ago
Floating and fleeting to and fro,
As in the well-remembered brook
They saw the inverted landscape gleam,
And their own faces like a dream
Look up upon them from below.

BIRDS OF PASSAGE

FLIGHT THE THIRD

85

FATA MORGANA

O SWEET illusions of Song,
    That tempt me everywhere,
In the lonely fields, and the throng
    Of the crowded thoroughfare!

I approach, and ye vanish away,
    I grasp you, and ye are gone;
But ever by night and by day,
    The melody soundeth on.

As the weary traveller sees
    In desert or prairie vast,
Blue lakes, overhung with trees,
    That a pleasant shadow cast;

Fair towns with turrets high,
    And shining roofs of gold,
That vanish as he draws nigh,
    Like mists together rolled,—

So I wander and wander along,
    And forever before me gleams
The shining city of song,
    In the beautiful land of dreams.

But when I would enter the gate
    Of that golden atmosphere,
It is gone, and I wander and wait
    For the vision to reappear.

THE HAUNTED CHAMBER

EACH heart has its haunted chamber,
  Where the silent moonlight falls!
On the floor are mysterious footsteps,
  There are whispers along the walls!

And mine at times is haunted
  By phantoms of the Past,
As motionless as shadows
  By the silent moonlight cast.

A form sits by the window,
  That is not seen by day,
For as soon as the dawn approaches
  It vanishes away.

It sits there in the moonlight,
  Itself as pale and still,
And points with its airy anger
  Across the window-sill.

Without, before the window,
  There stands a gloomy pine,
Whose boughs wave upward and downward
  As wave these thoughts of mine.

And underneath its branches
  Is the grave of a little child,
Who died upon life's threshold,
  And never wept nor smiled.

What are ye, O pallid phantoms!
    That haunt my troubled brain?
That vanish when day approaches,
    And at night return again?

What are ye, O pallid phantoms!
    But the statues without breath,
That stand on the bridge overarching
    The silent river of death?

THE MEETING

AFTER So long an absence
    At last we meet again :
Does the meeting give us pleasure,
    Or does it give us pain?

The tree of life has been shaken,
    And but few of us linger now,
Like the Prophet's two or three berries
    In the top of the uppermost bough.

We cordially greet each other
    In the old, familiar tone;
And we think, though we do not say it,
    How old and gray he is grown!

We speak of a Merry Christmas
    And many a Happy New Year;
But each in his heart is thinking
    Of those that are not here.

We speak of friends and their fortunes,
    And of what they did and said,
Till the dead alone seem living,
    And the living alone seem dead.

And at last we hardly distinguish
    Between the ghosts and the guests;
And a mist and shadow of sadness
    Steals over our merriest jests.

VOX POPULI

WHEN Mazárvan the Magician,
    Journeyed westward through Cathay,
Nothing heard he but the praises
    Of Badoura on his way.

But the lessening rumor ended
    When he came to Khaledan,
There the folk were talking only
    Of Prince Camaralzaman.

So it happens with the poets:
    Every province hath its own;
Camaralzaman is famous
    Where Badoura is unknown.

THE CASTLE-BUILDER

A GENTLE boy, with soft and silken locks,
    A dreamy boy, with brown and tender cycs,
A castle-builder, with his wooden blocks,
    And towers that touch imaginary skies.

A fearless rider on his father's knee,
    An eager listener unto stories told
At the Round Table of the nursery,
    Of heroes and adventures manifold.

There will be other towers for thee to build;
    There will be other steeds for thee to ride;
There will be other legends, and all filled
    With greater marvels and more glorified.

Build on, and make thy castles high and fair,
    Rising and reaching upward to the skies;
Listen to voices in the upper air,
    Nor lose thy simple faith in mysteries.

CHANGED

FROM the outskirts of the town,
    Where of old the mile-stone stood,
Now a stranger, looking down
I behold the shadowy crown
    Of the dark and haunted wood.

Is it changed, or am I changed?
    Ah! the oaks are fresh and green,
But the friends with whom I ranged
Through their thickets are estranged
    By the years that intervene.

Bright as ever flows the sea,
    Bright as ever shines the sun,
But alas! they seem to me
Not the sun that used to be,
    Not the tides that used to run.

THE CHALLENGE

I HAVE a vague remembrance
    Of a story, that is told
In some ancient Spanish legend
    Or chronicle of old.

It was when brave King Sanchez
    Was before Zamora slain,
And his great besieging army
    Lay encamped upon the plain.

Don Diego de Ordoñez
    Sallied forth in front of all,
And shouted loud his challenge
    To the warders on the wall.

All the people of Zamora,
    Both the born and the unborn,
As traitors did he challenge
    With taunting words of scorn.

The living, in their houses,
    And in their graves, the dead!
And the waters of their rivers,
    And their wine, and oil, and bread!

There is a greater army,
    That besets us round with strife,
A starving, numberless army,
    At all the gates of life.

The poverty-stricken millions
    Who challenge our wine and bread,
And impeach us all as traitors,
    Both the living and the dead.

And whenever I sit at the banquet,
    Where the feast and song are high,
Amid the mirth and the music
    I can hear that fearful cry.

And hollow and haggard faces
    Look into the lighted hall,
And wasted hands are extended
    To catch the crumbs that fall.

For within there is light and plenty,
    And odors fill the air;
But without there is cold and darkness,
    And hunger and despair.

And there in the camp of famine,
    In wind and cold and rain,
 Christ, the great Lord of the army,
    Lies dead upon the plain!

THE BROOK AND THE WAVE

THE brooklet came from the mountain,
　　As sang the bard of old,
Running with feet of silver
　　Over the sands of gold!

Far away in the briny ocean
　　There rolled a turbulent wave,
Now singing along the sea-beach,
　　Now howling along the cave.

And the brooklet has found the billow,
　　Though they flowed so far apart,
And has filled with its freshness and sweetness
　　That turbulent, bitter heart!

FROM THE SPANISH CANCIONEROS

1.

EYES so tristful, eyes so tristful,
Heart so full of care and cumber,
I was lapped in rest and slumber,
Ye have made me wakeful, wistful!

In this life of labore endless
Who shall comfort my distresses?
Querulous my soul and friendless
In its sorrow shuns caresses.
Ye have made me, ye have made me
Querulous of you, that care not,
Eyes so tristful, yet I dare not
Say to what ye have betrayed me.

2.

Some day, some day,
O troubled breast,
Shalt thou find rest.

If Love in thee
To grief give birth,
Six feet of earth
Can more than be;
There calm and free
And unoppressed
Shalt thou find rest.

The unattained
In life, at last
When life is passed,
Shall all be gained;
And no more pained,
No more distressed
Shalt thou find rest.

3.

Come, O Death, so silent flying
That unheard thy coming be,
Lest the sweet delight of dying
Bring life back again to me.

For thy sure approach perceiving
In my constancy and pain
I new life should win again,
Thinking that I am not living.
So to me, unconscious lying,
All unknown thy coming be,
Lest the sweet delight of dying
Bring life back again to me.

Unto him who finds thee hateful,
Death, thou art inhuman pain;
But to me, who dying gain,
Life is but a task ungrateful.
Come, then, with my wish complying,
All unheard thy coming be,
Lest the sweet delight of dying
Bring life back again to me.

4.

Glove of black in white hand bare,
And about her forehead pale
Wound a thin, transparent veil,
That doth not conceal her hair;
Sovereign attitude and air,
Cheek and neck alike displayed,
With coquettish charms arrayed,
Laughing eyes and fugitive;—
This is killing men that live,
'Tis not mourning for the dead.

AFTERMATH

WHEN the Summer fields are mown,
When the birds are fledged and flown,
    And the dry leaves strew the path;
With the falling of the snow,
With the cawing of the crow,
Once again the fields we mow
    And gather in the aftermath.

Not the sweet, new grass with flowers
  Is this harvesting of ours;
    Not the upland clover bloom;
But the rowen mixed with weeds,
Tangled tufts from marsh and meads,
Where the poppy drops its seeds
    In the silence and the gloom.

ABOUT THE AUTHOR

Henry Wadsworth Longfellow (1807-1882) was an American poet and educator. His best-known original works include "Paul Revere's Ride," "The Song of Hiawatha" and "Evangeline." He was the first American to completely translate Dante Alighieri's "Divine Comedy" and was one of the fireside poets from New England.

Longfellow wrote many lyric poems known for their musicality and often presenting stories of mythology and legend. He became the most popular American poet of  his day and had success overseas. He has been criticized for imitating European styles and writing poetry that was too sentimental.

1807

—February 27, 1807: Birth of Henry Wadsworth Longfellow at Portland, Maine (which was at that time still part of Massachusetts). He was the son of Stephen Longfellow, a lawyer, and Zilch Wadsworth, daughter of Peleg Wadsworth, a general in the American Revolutionary War and a member of Congress. His mother was descended from Richard Warren, who was a passenger on the Mayflower. His Mayflower ancestors also included William Brewster and John and Priscilla Alden.

1810

—Longfellow att4ends a dame school at age three.
1812
—April 30: Louisiana becomes the 18th state to j
—June 18: The War of 1812 begins, during which the United States
of America and its indigenous allies fought against the
United Kingdom and its allies in British North America.

1813

—Longfellow is enrolled at age six at the private Portland Academy.
—A naval battle occurs between American and British sips offshore
of New England. The treaty restored diplomatic relations
and restored the pre-war borders of June 1812.

1814

—December 24: The Treaty of Ghent, a peace treaty concluding
the War of 1812, was signed at Ghent, in the Netherlands,
by representatives of the United States and the United
Kingdom.

1816

—The statehood of Indiana is recognized, and Indiana becomes
the 19th state of the Union. Indiana had previously been
part of the Northwest Territory organized in 1787.

1817

—December 10: Mississippi becomes the 20th state admitted to
the Union of the United States. Mississippi seceded from
the Union and was restored to the Union in 1870, after the
American Civil War.

1818

—Illinois achieved statehood after being part of the Northwest
Territory for many years, becoming the 21st state of the
Union.

1819

—December The statehood of Alabama is recognized. Alabama would later secede from the Union in 1861, rejoining the Union in 1868 after the American Civil War.

1820

—March 15: Maine becomes the 23rd state of the United States, as part of the Missouri Compromise, after residents voted to secede from the Commonwealth of Massachusetts.
—Longfellow's first poem, "The Battle of Lovell's Pond," was published in the Portland Gazette on November 17, 1820. It was a patriotic and historical four-stanza poem.
—Nathaniel Hawthorne enrolls at Bowdoin College.

1821

—The former Missouri Territory is admitted to the Union as a slave state as part of the Missouri Compromise. Although the Confederacy recognized Missouri as its twelfth state, the secession was disputed and later regarded as not in effect.

1822

—Longfellow enrolls at Bowdoin College in Brunswick, Maine, along with his brother Stephen. His grandfather was a founder of the college and his father was a trustee. Here he met Nathaniel Hawthorne, a lifelong friend.

1824

—Nearly 40 minor poems by Longfellow are published between January 1824 and his graduation in 1825, many of these at the short-lived Boston periodical, The United States Literary Gazette."

1825

—Longfellow graduates from Bowdoin College, fourth in his class and elected to Phi Beta Kappa. He gave the student commencement address.

—Longfellow is offered a job as professor of modern languages at his alma mater, on condition that he prepare by touring Europe and learning Romance languages.

1826

—January 30: Washington Irving, while living in Paris, is invited to travel to Madrid to inspect the Spanish archives in the library of the American consul.

—In May, Longfellow travels from New York to Le Havre, in France, aboard the ship 'Cadmus.' He spent three years in Europe, visiting France, Spain, Italy, Germany, and England. During his time abroad he learned French, Italian, Spanish, Portuguese, and German, mostly without formal instruction. While in Madrid, he met with Washington Irving, who encouraged his writing.

—July 4: Former U.S. Presidents Thomas Jefferson and John Adams both die on the 50th anniversary of the signing of the United States Declaration of Independence.

1827

—In the United Kingdom, George Canning succeeds Lord Liverpool as British prime minister.

—The term "socialist" is coined by Robert Owen in his London periodical, The Co-operative Magazine and Monthly Herald.

1828

—January: Washington Irving's book, "A History of the Life and Voyages of Christopher Columbus," was published.

—The first substantial praise of Longfellow's work is published, by John Neal, a fellow native of Portland, Maine, in the January 23, 1828 issue of his magazine, "The Yankee." He

wrote: "As for Mr. Longfellow, he has a fine genius and a pure and safe taste,..."
—December 3: Andrew Jackson is elected President of the United States, defeating incumbent John Quincy Adams.

1829

—March 22; Greece receives autonomy from the Ottoman Empire.
—July 23: In the United States, William Burt obtains the first patent for a form of typewriter, the typographer.
—In mid-August, Longfellow returns to the United States.
—August 27: Longfellow wrote to the president of Bowdoin that he was turning down the professorship because he considered the $600 salary "disproportionate to the duties required." The trustees raised his salary to $800 with an additional $100 to serve as the college's librarian, which required one hour of work per day. While teaching at the college he translated textbooks from French, Italian, and Spanish.

1831

—July 21: Leopold of Saxe-Coburg-Gotha is inaugurated as the first King of the Belgians in Brussels.
—September 14, Longfellow marries Mary Storer, a childhood friend from Portland, Maine.

1832

—February 28: Charles Darwin and the crew of HMS Beagle arrive at South America for the first time.
—Greece is recognized as a sovereign nation by the Treaty of Constantinople, ending the Greek War of Independence.

1833

—Washington Irving's book, "Tales of the Alhambra," a book of short stories, is published.
—Longfellow's first published book was a translation of poetry

by the medieval Spanish poet, Jorge Manrique, "Coplas de Don Jorge Manrique."
—Publication of several nonfiction and fiction prose pieces inspired by Irving, including "The Indian Summer" and "The Bald Eagle."

1834

—Longfellow receives a letter from Harvard College offering him the Smith Professorship of Modern Languages, with the stipulation that he spend a year abroad. He and his wife travel to Europe, where he studies German as well as Dutch, Danish, Swedish, Finnish, and Icelandic.
—The Spanish Inquisition, which had begun in the 15th century, is suppressed by royal decree.

1835

—Publication of "Outer-Mer: A Pilgrimage Beyond the Sea," a collection of Prose works by Longfellow. The term "outer-mer" is French for "overseas."
—September 7: Charles Darwin arrives at the Galapagos Islands, aboard HMS Beagle.
—November 29: Death of Longfellow's first wife, after a miscarriage. Her body was shipped home to the United States for burial at Mount Auburn Cemetery near Boston.
—December 28: The Second Seminole War led by Osceola breaks out.

1836

—Longfellow returns to the United States and assumes the professorship at Harvard.
—June 15: Arkansas is the 25th state admitted into the United States of America. Arkansas seceded from the Union in 1861 and rejoined in 186, after the American Civil War.
—Sam Houston is elected as the first president of the Republic of Texas.

1837

—January 26: Michigan becomes the 26th state of the United States, following the Toledo War, a boundary dispute with Ohio, in which Ohio was granted the Toledo region and Michigan was given the western part of the Upper Peninsula.

—During the spring Longfellow has rented rooms at the Craigie House, built in 1759, which served as the headquarters of George Washington during the Siege of Boston. Previous boarders included Jared Sparks, Edward Everett, and Joseph Emerson Worcester. The house is preserved as the Longfellow House-Washington's Headquarters National Historic Site.

—Charles Dickens's "Oliver Twist" begins publication in serial form in London.

1838

—Longfellow writes the poem, "Footsteps of Angels," said to be about his late wife.

—June 28: The coronation of Queen Victoria takes place at Westminster Abbey in London.

—July 4: The Iowa Territory is formally established after a bill signed by U.S. President Martin Van Buren on June 12.

1839

—Publication of Longfellow's first poetry collection, "Voices of the Night," his first book of poetry. Although most of the book was translations, it included nine original poems and seven poems that he had written as a teenager.

—During Longfellow's seven-year long courtship of Frances "Fanny" Appleton, whose family lived at Beacon Hill in Boston. He often walked from Cambridge to the Appleton home by crossing the Boston Bridge. That bridge was replaced in 1906 with a new bridge later renamed as the Longfellow Bridge.

—Publication of "Hyperion: A Romance," a romance novel, whose main character, Paul Flemming, travels through Germany and falls in love with an Englishwoman who rejects him. The semi-autobiographical novel hints of his own travels, his atheistic beliefs and his own as yet unsuccessful courtship. The novel's descriptions of Germany would later inspire its use as a companion travel guide for American tourists in that country.

1840?

—Longfellow takes a six-month leave of absence from Harvard to attend a health spa in the former Marienberg Benedictine Convent at Boppard in Germany

1841

—Publication of Longfellow's "Ballads and Other Poems," which included "The Village Blacksmith" and "The Wreck of the Hesperus."
—January 26: Britain occupies Hong Kong, an island with a population of 7,500.
—March 4: William Henry Harrison is sworn in as the ninth President of the United States.
—April 6: John Tyler is sworn in as the tenth President of the United States, two days after Harrison's death of pneumonia.

1842

—Publication of the drama "The Spanish Student: A Play in Three Acts," a play in which he reflects on his time in Spain in the 1820s.
—Publication of Longfellow's "Poems on Slavery," his first public support of abolitionism and anti-slavery efforts. Most of the poems were written at sea in October 1842. The poems were later reprinted as anti-slavery tracts in 1843, and included: "To William E. Channing," "The Slave's Dream," "The Good Part," "The Slave in the Dismal Swamp," "The Slave

Singing at Midnight," "The Witnesses," "The Quadroon Girl," and "The Warning."

1843

—Longfellow marries Frances Elizabeth Appleton.
—Nathan Appleton, the father of Longfellow's wife, purchases the former Craigie house as a wedding present, and Longfellow lives there for the rest of his life.

1844

—Birth of Charles Appleton Longfellow
—Publication of "Poets and Poetry of Europe," with translations by Longfellow.

1845

—March 3: Florida is admitted to the Union as the 27th state. Florida, an area previously contested by Spain and Great Britain, had been ceded to the United States in 1819. Florida seceded from the Union in 1861 and rejoined in 1868, after the American Civil War.
—March 4: James K. Polk (1795-1849) is sworn in as the 11th president of the United States of America.
—Birth of Ernest Wadsworth Longfellow
—Publication of "The Belfry of Bruges and Other Poems," a poetry collection.
—Publication of "The Waif: A Collection of Poems," an anthology of poems by various authors, to which Longfellow contributed "Proem."
—December 29: Texas is recognized as the 28th state of the United States.

1846

—December 28, 1846: Iowa becomes the 29th state in the Union.

1847

—April 7: Birth of Fanny Longfellow, the Longfellows' first daughter. During childbirth, Dr. Nathan Cooley Keep administered ether to the mother as the first obstetric anesthetic in the United States.

—November 1: Publication of Longfellow's epic poem, "Evangeline: A Tale of Acadia."

1848

—May 29: Wisconsin becomes the 30th state to join the United States.

1849

—Publication of "Kavanagh: A Tale," a story of a country romance, in which Mr. Churchill, a school teacher, who has always planned to write a romance, but whose procrastination has never allowed him to start, until late in life he resigns himself to his "destiny."

—March 4: Major General Zachary Taylor (1784-1850) is sworn in as the 12th president of the United States of America.

1850

—Birth of Alice Mary Longfellow

—Publication of "The Seaside and the Fireside," a poetry collection.

—March 4: Millard Fillmore (1800-1874) is sworn in as the 13th president of the United States.

1851

—Publication of "The Golden Legend," a poem.

1852

—Publication of "The Poetical Works of Henry Wadsworth Longfellow," a poetry collection, in London, with illustrations by John Gilbert.

1853

—Birth of Edith Longfellow
—March 4: Franklin Pierce (1804-1869) is sworn in as the 14th president of the United States of America.
—June 13: Longfellow hosts a farewell dinner party at his Cambridge home for his friend Nathaniel Hawthorne, who was preparing to move overseas.

1854

—Longfellow retired from his teaching position at Harvard to focus on his writing

1855

—Birth of Anne Allegra Longfellow
—Publication of "The Song of Hiawatha," an epic poem in trochaic tetrameter, featuring Native American characters. The epic tells the fictional adventures of an Ojibwe warrior named Hiawatha and the tragedy of his love for Minnehaha, a Dakota woman.

1857

—March 4: James Buchanan (1791-1868) is sworn in as the 15th president of the United States of America.

1858

—May 11: The Minnesota Territory is admitted to the Union as the 32nd state in the United States.
—Publication of "The Courtship of Miles Standish and Other Poems," a poetry collection. "The Courtship of Miles Standish" is a narrative poem, written in dactylic hexameter, about the early days of Plymouth Colony, the colonial settlement established in America by the Mayflower pilgrims. The poem was among the most enduringly popular of Longfellow's works.

1859

—February 14: Oregon is admitted to the Union as the 33rd state of the United States.

—Longfellow is awarded an honorary doctorate of laws from Harvard.

1860

—April 6: Longfellow writes the poem, "Paul Revere's Ride," commemorating the actions of Paul Revere on April 18, 1775, when he was said to warn American patriot defenders of the approaching British, although not a historically accurate account. It was written the day after Longfellow visited the Old North Church in Boston and climbed its tower It was first published in the January 1861 issue of 'The Atlantic Monthly.' Longfellow's family was said to have a connection to the historical Paul Revere in that his maternal grandfather, Peleg Wadsworth, had been Revere's commander during the Penobscot Expedition.

1861

—January 29: Kansas becomes the 39th state to join the United States.

—March 4: Abraham Lincoln (1809-1865) is sworn in as the 16th president of the United States of America.

—April 12: Start of the American Civil War, in which the Union states and the states of the southern Confederacy fought over issues of slavery.

—July 9: Longfellow's wife was sealing an envelope with hot sealing wax, or lighting a match, when her dress caught fire and her body was badly burned.

—July 10: Death of Francis Appleton, Longfellow's wife.

—Death of Longfellow's second wife, after sustaining burns when her dress caught fire. The distraught Longfellow was himself was injured by burns on his face, after trying to quench the flames with his body, and after that wore a beard to conceal the scars.

1863

—January 1: The Emancipation Proclamation was a presidential proclamation and executive order issued by Abraham Lincoln granted freedom to the slaves of the Confederacy.

—June 20: West Virginia is admitted to the Union as the 35th state of the United States, after seceding from the Confederate State of Virginia.

—July 1-3: The Battle of Gettysburg, fought near the town of Gettysburg in Pennsylvania, in which Union forces halted the Confederates' invasion to the north, was considered a turning point of the American Civil War.

—Publication of "The Legend of Rabbi Ben Levi," a poem telling about Yehoshua ben Levi, a Jewish rabbi and scholar of the Talmud who lived in the land of Israel in the first half of the third century, and taught in the city of Lod, and was known for his debates of theological matters.

—November 23: Publication of "Tales of a Wayside Inn," a poetry collection, in which a group of people gathered at the Wayside Inn in Sudbury, Massachusetts, (about 20 miles from the poet's home in Cambridge), each take turns each telling a story in a variety of poetic forms and styles. The characters are said to be loosely based on actual persons of Longfellow's acquaintance. Includes his previously published poem, "Paul Revere's Ride," and "The Saga of King Olaf." Includes the "second flight" of "Birds of Passage").

—December 25: Longfellow writes the poem "Christmas Bells," which becomes the lyrics of the beloved Christmas carol, "I Heard the Bells on Christmas Day."

1864

—Longfellow launches the "Dante Club," of friends who meet weekly to help with perfecting the translation of Dante Alighieri's "Divine Comedy." Guests included regulars

William Dean Howells, James Russell Lowell, and Charles Eliot Norton.

—October 31: Nevada becomes the 36th state of the Union.

1865

—Longfellow's poem, "Christmas Bells," is published in "Our Young Folks," a juvenile magazine published by Ticknor and Fields.

—Publication of "Household Poems," a poetry collection.

—April 9: Confederate General Robert E. Lee surrenders to Union General Ulysses S. Grant after the Battle of Appomattox Court House.

—April 15: Andrew Johnson (1808-1875) is sworn in as the 17th president of the United States of America, following the assassination of Abraham Lincoln.

1867

—March 1: Nebraska becomes the 37th state of the Union.

—Publication of "The Divine Comedy," Longfellow's translation of Dante Alighieri's work, in three volumes, although revisions continued and the work went through four printings in the first year.

—Publication of "Flower-de-Luce," a poetry collection.

1868

—Publication of "The New England Tragedies," containing two dramatic plays in verse reflecting on events in the early days of New England. The play "John Endicott" dramatizes the clash between the Puritans and the Quakers and the play "Giles Corey of the Salem Farms" is about the Salem witchcraft trials.

1869

—March 4: General Ulysses S. Grant (1822-1885) is sworn in as the 18th president of the United States of America.

1871

—Publication of Longfellow's translation of Dante Alighieri's "The Divine Tragedy," in three volumes.

1872

—Publication of "Christus: A Mystery," a trilogy composed of three previous works: "The Golden Legend," The New England Tragedies," and "The Divine Tragedy."
—Publication of "Three Books of Song," a poetry collection (including the second part of "Tales of a Wayside Inn").
—Longfellow's poem, "Christmas Bells," is set to music by the English organist, John Baptiste Calkin, using a melody called "Waltham." Other melodies have been used, including the 1845 melody of "Mainzer" and a 1956 tune by Johnny Marks, which was popularized by a Bing Crosby recording.

1873

—Publication of "Aftermath," (comprising the third part of "Tales of a Wayside Inn," and the "third flight" of "Birds of Passage").

1874

—Samuel Ward helped Longfellow with the selling of a poem, "The Hanging of the Crane," to the 'New York Ledger' for $3,000, the highest price ever paid for a poem.
—Longfellow oversees the publication of a 31-volume anthology, called "Poems of Places," which collected poems representing geographical locations, including European, Asian, and Arabian countries.

1875

—Publication of "The Masque of Pandora and Other Poems," a poetry collection.

1876

—August 1: Colorado is admitted to the Union, after being organized as the Territory of Colorado since 1861.

1877

—March 4: Rutherford B. Hayes (1822-1893) is sworn in as the 19th president of the United States of America.

1878

—Publication of "Kêramos and Other Poems," a poetry collection.

1880

—Publication of "Ultima Thule," a poetry collection.

1881

—March 4: James A. Garfield ((1831-1881) is sworn in as the 20th president of the United States of America.

1882

—March 24: Death of Longfellow at his home in Cambridge, surrounded by family. He is buried at Mount Auburn Cemetery in Cambridge, Massachusetts.
—Publication of "In the Harbor," a poetry collection.

—Publication of "Michael Angelo: A Fragment," (incomplete, published posthumously).